Place your
BETS

John Goodwin

Published in association with
The Basic Skills Agency

Hodder & Stoughton

A MEMBER OF THE HODDER HEADLINE GROUP

Acknowledgements
Cover: Louise Hilton, NB Illustration
Illustrations: Jo Blake

Orders: please contact Bookpoint Ltd, 130 Milton Park, Abingdon, Oxon OX14
4SB. Telephone: (44) 01235 827720, Fax: (44) 01235 400454. Lines are open from
9.00 – 6.00, Monday to Saturday, with a 24 hour message answering service.

British Library Cataloguing in Publication Data
A catalogue record for this title is available from The British Library

ISBN 0 340 86950 X

First published 2001
This edition published 2002
Impression number   10 9 8 7 6 5 4 3 2 1
Year   2007 2006 2005 2004 2003 2002

Copyright © 2001 John Goodwin

Typeset by SX Composing DTP, Rayleigh, Essex
Printed in Great Britain for Hodder & Stoughton Educational, a division of Hodder
Headline Plc, 338 Euston Road, London NW1 3BH by Athenaeum Press,
Gateshead, Tyne and Wear

About the play

The People
- **Emma**   aged 17
- **Carla**   her sister aged 15
- **Mum**   their mother

The Scene
Emma *and* **Carla** *have just come home from school.*

They are waiting for their mum to come back from work.

Act 1

Carla	It isn't there.
Emma	Look again.
Carla	I have looked again.
Emma	Maybe it's hidden under something.
Carla	I've looked under everything.
Emma	Maybe you took it to Sam's.
Carla	I didn't take it to Sam's.
Emma	Are you sure?
Carla	Emma my CD player has gone.
	We've had a break in, Emma.
Emma	A break in?
Carla	Yes.
Emma	We haven't had a break in.
Carla	Then where's the TV gone?
Emma	What?
Carla	The TV has gone.
	Look for yourself.

They go into the kitchen.

Emma   Oh yes.

Carla   Somebody has broken into the house.
They've nicked my CD player and
the TV.

*Emma is still looking at the space where
the TV was.*

Emma   No they haven't.

Carla   They must have.

Emma   Er . . . no. The TV had to go back to
the shop.

Carla   What?

Emma   Yeah . . . it had to go in for repair.

Carla   What was wrong with it?

Emma   The sound had gone.

Carla   It was working perfectly yesterday.

Emma   Carla, I am telling you the TV
has gone in for repair OK?

Carla   No it is not OK.

Emma	I can't stand about arguing, Carla.
	I have to get the tea ready.
	Mum will be home soon.
Carla	But what about my CD player?
Emma	I've already said you must have left
	it at Sam's.
	Go round there and check it out.
Carla	It will be a waste of time.
Emma	Carla, just go.

Act 2

Half an hour later

Mum	My feet are killing me.
Emma	Mum, we need to talk.
Mum	I've been on my feet all day.
Emma	Mum.
Mum	Friday is such a busy day.
Emma	You've been up to your tricks again, haven't you?
Mum	Still it's a nice tea you've made Emma.
Emma	Don't try and change the subject.
Mum	I'm not changing the subject.
Emma	Where's the TV gone?
Mum	What?
Emma	And Carla's CD player?
Mum	I don't know what you're talking about.
Emma	Yes you do.

	You've been gambling again haven't you?
Mum	I have not.
Emma	Scratch cards is it?
Mum	No.
Emma	Betting on the horses?
Mum	No.
Emma	How much money did you lose?
Mum	I haven't lost any money.
Emma	Yes you have. That's why you sold Carla's CD player and the TV.
Mum	I haven't been gambling.
Emma	How could you? Your own daughter's CD player.
Mum	I haven't done anything.
Emma	Yes you have. Tell the truth, Mum.
Mum	It's only temporary.
Emma	So you took them down the second-hand shop.
Mum	I needed a bit of cash.

	I got a good tip for the horses.
Emma	But the horse lost.
Mum	Yes.
Emma	You said you'd never gamble again.
Mum	This was different, Emma.
Emma	You promised me.
Mum	I'll get her CD player back. I'll get the TV back.
Emma	What are you going to use for money?
Mum	I'll get them both back. It'll be easy.
Emma	Oh yeah. Like last time?

Act 3

Later that night. **Carla** *is looking at her CD player.*

Emma   So there it is.

Carla   Yes.

Emma   It was here all the time.

Carla   Where did you find it?

Emma   In your bedroom.

Carla   I looked in my bedroom.

Emma   Did you?

Carla   Yes.

Emma   Well I found it.

Carla   What's this scratch on it?

Emma   What scratch?

Carla   This big scratch here. Look.
There's a bit that's been smashed
off as well.

Emma	It must have always been like that.
Carla	You're a liar, Emma.
Emma	Don't call me a liar.
Carla	You're not telling me the truth.
Emma	What do you mean?
Carla	Something's happened to my CD player. I want to know what you've done to it.
Emma	I've done nothing to it.
Carla	Tell me the truth.
Emma	Right, I will.
Carla	Come on then.
Emma	It's Mum. She sold it down the second-hand shop.
Carla	What?
Emma	For money to go gambling with.
Carla	What are you talking about?
Emma	She's an addict, Carla. Like some people are drug addicts. Mum is a gambling addict.

Carla	She never is.
Emma	Oh yes.
	She sold the TV for money
	to go gambling with.
Carla	No.
Emma	Oh yes.
Carla	I don't believe you.
Emma	You remember the holiday we were
	going on?
Carla	Yeah.
Emma	We didn't go because she spent the
	money on betting on the horses.
Carla	Why didn't you tell me?
Emma	She didn't want you to know about
	it. I got your CD player back.
Carla	How did you do that?
Emma	With the money I saved from my
	Saturday job.
Carla	Emma . . .
Emma	But I can't do it any more Carla.

Carla	Where is she?
Emma	She's gone to the pub.
	When she gets back we've got to sort her out.
	I can't do it myself.
	I need you to help me.
	Will you help me?

Act 4

An hour later.

Mum   What's this then?

Emma   We need to talk to you.

Don't we, Carla?

Carla   Yeah.

Mum   Can't it wait till tomorrow?

Emma   No it can't.

Mum   But it's late.

We've all got to be up early in the morning.

Emma   It won't take long.

Mum   Go on then if you must.

Emma   Right . . . well . . . go on Carla.

Carla   You say it, Emma.

Emma   But you said you'd start it off.

Mum	Come on.
Emma	We want you to give up gambling.
Mum	Is this what all this fuss is about?
Carla	Yeah.
Mum	Look I've said I've given it up OK?
Emma	No Mum. You've said that before.
Mum	Oh come on Emma.
	I need to get to bed.
Emma	No Mum. This time it's for real.
	We come home from school.
	The TV and Carla's CD player are
	missing.
Mum	I said it won't happen again.
Emma	How many times have you
	said that?
	I've lost count.
	What will it be next time?
	The kitchen table? Our own beds?
	All our clothes?
	I've lost all my savings
	because of you.
Mum	I said I'm sorry.

Emma	That's not enough.
	I worked every Saturday for that
	cash and now I haven't got a penny.
Mum	I'll pay it back.
Emma	Oh yeah.
Mum	Really I will.
Carla	We've decided, Mum.
Mum	Decided what?
Carla	If you do it again we're going.
Mum	Where would you go to?
Emma	We'd go to Dad's house.
Mum	You wouldn't do that.
Carla	Yes, we would.
Mum	He'd never have you.
Carla	He would.
Emma	So we're telling you straight, Mum.
	No second chances.
Carla	We'll be out of here fast.
Emma	So now you know.
	It's gambling or us.
	You choose.

Act 5

Three weeks later. **Mum** *enters carrying a big cardboard box.*

Mum	Mind out the way Carla. I need to put this down.
Carla	What have you got there?
Mum	Just move.

She puts the box down.

Emma	What have you got?
Mum	Go on Carla open the box.

Carla *opens the box.*

Emma	What is it?
Carla	It's a TV.

Mum	It's our TV. I got it back from the shop.
Carla	Great!
Emma	Where did you get the money from?
Mum	From my wages. I saved up.
Emma	Right.
Mum	I'll pay you back, Emma. Next week. I should manage it by next week.

Carla takes the TV out of the box and plugs it in.

Carla	Just in time to watch the football.
Mum	Things are sorted. Back on the way up.
Carla:	Yeah.
Mum	I've given up gambling for good.
Emma	Yeah.

Act 6

Two weeks later

Mum   There you are Emma, sixty pounds.

Emma   Really?

Mum   Yes. You count it.
That's all I owe you.

Emma   Thanks.

Mum   There's a present for you Carla . . .
here.

Carla   Great!

Mum   Maybe you could buy yourself a
CD with it.

Carla   Wow! Thirty quid.
I can buy two with this.

Mum   Why not? And I thought we
could go on holiday.
To make up for the one
we missed in the summer.

Emma	You've given me seventy pounds.
Mum	What?
Emma	You owed me sixty.
	But you've given me seventy.
Mum	Well keep it anyway.
Emma	Where did you get all this money from?
Mum	I got a rise at work.
Emma	A rise?
Mum	Yes. A big one.
Emma	Really . . .
Mum	So where do you fancy for a holiday then Carla?
Emma	You're a liar, Mum.
Mum	Somewhere on a hot sunny beach, Carla? Soaking up the sun?
Emma	Carla . . .
Carla	What?
Emma	It's time we were going.
Carla	Going where?
Emma	We need to pack our things.
Carla	What?

Emma	We're going to Dad's.
Carla	What are you on about?
Emma	You've won on the horses haven't you Mother?
Mum	Of course I haven't.
Emma	There's no way a raise could pay for all this. You must think we're stupid.
Mum	I never thought that. I just wanted to give you some good things for once.
Emma	So you went back to gambling.
Mum	I won a thousand pounds.
Carla	How much?
Mum	Look it's all here.

She takes a thick bundle of notes out of her pocket.

Carla	I don't believe it.
Mum	I won the jackpot at bingo. Nobody's won it for three weeks. It was a roll over.

24

Carla	Look at all that cash.
Emma	And now you expect us to roll over.
Mum	It was just one game of bingo.
	It only cost me a couple of quid.
	Where's the harm in that?
Emma	You promised us no more gambling.
Carla	But we can go on holiday, Emma.
Emma	No.
Mum	I won't go again.
Emma	But you will. You will.
	This time you've won.
	But what about next time?
	And the time after that?
	You throw away your life on
	betting.
	On bingo. On the lottery.
	On scratch cards.
	On arcade games.
	Well I'm not going to see you do it.
	I'm going to Dad's.
Mum	No. Please Emma.
Emma	You can do what you like Carla but

	I'm going now.
Mum	No, Emma.

Emma ignores her mother.
She goes into her bedroom and begins to pack her
bag.

If you have enjoyed reading this book, you may be interested in other titles in the *Livewire* series.

The Library
Romeo, Romeo
Doing Macbeth
Night Fishing
Selling Out

The Mimic
Football Clones
The Tourists
The Chosen One